AF375130

DREAM *Boudoir*

A JOURNAL OF AMOROUS MUSINGS

DREAM Boudoir

A JOURNAL OF AMOROUS MUSINGS

Ætenos Publishing Company

Published by:

Ætenos Publishing Company
Wheaton, IL 60187

dreamboudoir@outlook.com

ISBN-10: 9798218279516

ISBN-13: 9798219279523

Library of Congress Control Number: 2023917065

Cover Design/Layout by L. Ean Adams

The Moment (p.151) by L. Ean Adams

Printed in USA

contents

*I write to remember
   the moments before the silence
lest the silence
   becomes the remembrance.*

whoever you are,
now with your eyes focused
on these simple missives
and those soon to follow,
i ask you to take my breath,
take these words,
let them linger.....

part one
of dreams and haiku

the dream of you near.
sweet earth soft and wet, our lips
conjoined in a dance.

my embarrassed cock.
blushing red at the slightest
touch of your sweet lips.

going down on you
summons the same lightning as
me shouting *shazam!*

i touched you and you
were so wet as i slid in
and out. exploding.

i woke at full mast.
the soft breeze from her lips guide
me to welcomed shores.

dew drops fall from her
sweet petals. wet sighs sing to
a soft tongue-licked earth.

her sweet lips perform
alchemy, transforming my
willing flesh to stone.

i breathe better in
your arms until your kisses
render me breathless.

her sighs were like a
treasure map guiding me to
the precious gemstone.

morning silence is
marred by the sound of her sighs
and my cock crowing.

bright stars peer through the
window. her flesh covers mine
in a satin dream.

her fertile valley.
ravaged by my desire,
replenished with my seeds.

i miss you. my lips
are sad, my arms are empty.
last night my cock wept.

the slightest flick of
her tongue builds a spark that
sets my wick on fire.

my cock spends most of
the day depressed. head down in
a solemn dangle.

her moist nothingness
cleanses in a baptism
of self-forgetting.

her precious heartbeat
against my own. the moonlight
colors our embrace.

she uses her tongue
like a dagger, slicing through
my rigidity.

my cock emerges from
dream, glazed by your wetness
in the morning sun.

sleeping desires
unmasked in bare flesh hasten
a dream convergence.

happiness is the
frequency of our bare flesh
touching in motion.

her lips descending,
drawing a wet sensual
line to the hard pause.

she cried out as my
tongue plunged deep, drowning in her
savage breakwaters.

my lips respond to
your lips. two heartbeats echo,
lost in the dreaming.

these sheets crumpled and
sweetly soiled, immortalized
by our desire.

i am alone. the
echoes of my desire
haunt this lonely place.

lying in that wet
spot coaxes hard remembrance
of you saying ooohhhh!

a fragrant river
issues from within her source
soon to be distilled.

she guides my head to
where the waters flow. narrow
gorge, raging river.

lust subsists without
love. the longevity of
love depends on lust.

i licked her rich dark
hummingbird style. tongue lapping
wild, tongue dancing deep.

bodies in motion.
sublime fragrance emerges
from the moist darkness.

sweet earth you welcome
me in your garden. i keep
your soil nice and wet.

beauty passes in
six feet of silence. strangers
to remain strangers.

-Covid/Lockdown inspired

months perfecting my
smile in anticipation
of her acceptance.

-Covid/Lockdown inspired

covid took my sense
of taste. your rich elixir
of life brought it back.

-Covid/Lockdown inspired

exquisite brew spills
from her cup. the tip of my
tongue stirring wildly.

the fragrance of our
bodies drenched in desire's
rapturous cleansing.

my hard cock rises
early. my homage to you
in the morning sun.

your wild hip movements
and tangy sauce send my tongue
into sheer madness.

it is because of
you that i have not lost hope
in humanity.

her inner beauty
excites. her outer beauty
is pure excitement.

watching you rise from
bed after our wondrous night
is a lovely thing.

sweet remembrance of
your exquisite kisses leave
me yearning for more.

my love for you made
evident with seventeen
syllables heart-inked.

your beautiful sighs
guide me in the dark to that
one star shining bright.

how she transforms my
solitude into a wild
rhythmic disorder.

lyrical notes of
skin resonance airing a
divine symphony.

kiss embrace undress
merge strain perspire exhale
hydrate sleep repeat

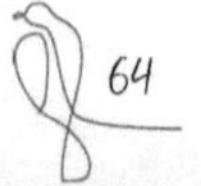

you represent the
words filling this page. there is
nothing else but you.

part two
moonlight whispers

her strange beautiful garden.
   barren of any foliage,
yet heavily scented
   and blossoming.

her mouth
forms an o,
encircling
in playful tease
coaxing
my mouth
into an o.

my hard desire is the fire
   scorching
her sugared lips

  as our bodies
become drenched
  in pure absinthe.

the streets were empty
   except for a car stopped at the intersection.

the people inside the car
   were suspended in a kiss.

the light was green.

fragrant honey drips
in moonlight flashes.

the reclusive bee
emerges from its dark place.

dreams of you awaken
  the fullness of my desire.

your sweet lips settle,
  closing my eyes again to dream.

outside
the snow falls resolutely

as the cold wind howls
        against the window.

inside
breath escapes into sighs

as an orchid blossoms
        underneath my warm embrace.

my desire rises
   as the morning sun
illuminates
      the room
where her hips
         begin to rise.

not a word sounds
    as she kneels
on the padded altar
    in a wordless prayer,
  an earnest benediction
awaiting my holy sacrament
    on the tip of her tongue.

she says yes
to my love
as her kisses
guide me
to the innermost
part of her heart.

her kisses
were like a lightning strike
    sending
        waves of electricity
    pulsating
            throughout my veins
    as i grounded
        a portion of my flesh
            for safety.

sighs echo
as wave after wave
crash onto the shore,
drenching the sand
hardened by desire's necessity.

an absence in-between
hides a secret oasis.

a burning desire
compels a parched wanderer
into the void.

every night i dream your image
deep into the bright stars
dancing in the dark sky.

and every night my desire strains upwards
dreaming of that single glistening star
illuminating your milky way convergence.

there is something
  about the way our lips touch.

my eyes close.

my soul melts.

your kiss transforms
  every part of my flesh into fire.

she transcribes
  the imaginary words
that i write
  on her flesh
using
  very
    precise
      mouth
        movements
  into vocal distillations
too obscene
    for the written word.

last night i lay
   with my imaginary lover.

i was naked and anxious.

she was fully clothed
   and unresponsive to my touch.

her flower blossoms
as two petals open wide.

sweet nectar flows perfectly
in a lips tongue pollination.

situated at the entrance
of her secret paradise,

i know i am exalted
to have been selected
as her chosen one.

now to be richly rewarded
for my unwavering devotion
and imminent misdeed.

i know that this loneliness
which has enveloped
my every thought,
my every breath
will soon fade.

but at this moment,
this hollow space without you
defines my aloneness
and makes the loneliness
seem unending.

there is no pleasure
    in the void itself.

it is the enclosing walls,
    moist and nurturing,

that give meaning
    to the nothingness.

all you can eat diner

the diner opens.

"welcome" is emblazoned in her eyes. she offers me
the daily special, her delicious all-you-can-eat buffet
arranged on a choice platter and seasoned exquisitely
just for me. i always dine to the point of sheer gluttony,
ravaging all of the delectable morsels prepared in her
small oven. there is never any reproachment on her part
for my unabashed appetites and poor table manners,
only the hope that i will return to her establishment
soon hungry for more.

framed in silence

the room has regained its silence.

the bed has stopped its thumping and creaking.

passionate moans no longer punctuate the air.

the wet flesh singing loudly in clang and clamor
has become mute.

her body is framed beautifully in my embrace
   as we drift soundlessly.

v.i.p. room

she told me that special privileges were needed to gain access to her exclusive v.i.p. room. so i set a reservation with a soft caress and well-articulated kisses knowing that in a few moments her special v.i.p. room, albeit small yet vast in its amenities and wonderment, will be wrecked rock star style.

goddess of love

you are my goddess
having taken on flesh
so that this mere mortal
can worship you in the flesh.
come,
lie with me
on this padded altar
where i can sing praises
to you with lips
tongue
cock
everything.

sacred

this moment with you is sacred.

the little piece of flesh that blesses the tip of my
tongue offers more spiritual nourishment than any
holy catechism.

your orgasm anointing my lips, immerses my soul
more completely in the divine than any church
ordained baptism.

hunger

the night has wandered deep into the late hour and
i am sitting here, my eyes washing over your image
again. my eyes are fixed on the picture of you highlight
in black; the picture of you wearing that sexy dress
which accentuates the fullness of your body perfectly
and gives such prominence to your delicious ass; the
sexy little dress that rides every curvaceous line of your
gorgeous body with such deliciously sinful precision -
imprisoning my thoughts in a feverishly insane reverie
and provoking a blood surge that makes my slumber-
ing desire awaken and quiver in anticipation.

i long for that moment when our naked bodies reveal
themselves again as we breathe each other completely
breathless until the rapturous effluence and then sweet
exhaustion. i yearn for the rich intensity, the plenitude,
the sweet nourishment of the transformative waters
that flow from within your magical gardenia.

everyday i hunger to be purified and reborn in your
nectar-laden paradise.

our biblical intimacy

our biblical intimacy.

my miraculous staff
        raised high
        to part the divide.

your glistening bush
        illuminating
        the way to paradise.

my unapologetic addiction

lying face down
with my head lodged
between your legs
has become
my unapologetic addiction -
having overdosed
many times
on the pure opium
that flows.

always

   lying in bed with you last night
holding you close in my arms while you slept,
you were so calm.
      so peaceful.
       so beautiful.

but every so often you would jump,
   shudder,
and i wondered what demons
had infiltrated your dreams.

   and each time you trembled,
i held you closer to me
      delicately caressing your hair
   and softly pressing my lips to yours
which always calmed the unquiet fears.

and i realized as a solitary tear
   traced a line across my face,
that i wanted to be there holding you,
     caressing you,
      kissing you,
       protecting you......

    always.

without you

this bedroom
        without you
                is barren -

an arid confinement
        thirsting
                for the amorous drenching

that only you
        can provide.

unknown

i am unknown, a mere microcosmic fragment in this seemingly infinite world of possibilities. i am alone in hatred of this all-encompassing loneliness that has supplanted the happiness of my days and left my nights unencumbered of any passionate moments.

so many beautiful women pass daily - never looking, never stopping, never even hesitating. and i watch them all hoping for a quick glance to provide tacit assurance that i exist or just a single word to assuage this ache, this deep longing, this restlessness to which i have been shackled.

but there is no comfort, no respite to settle this storm and stress where i wait for something marvelous to become manifest in my life - waiting for that moment when she and i finally discover each other, and her closeness dispels this loneliness creating a perfect solace in her arms.

weary of dreams

i choose to sleep just a few hours each night because
why should the dream of you be richer, more beautiful
than the waking reality? why should i offer morpheus,
the god of dreams, more of you than what has been
allotted to me?

i am weary of dreams, these chimerical teasings with
their fantastical offerings of ephemeral flesh and
phantom embraces that always vanish upon waking.
i have dreamt you enough and now every part of me
aches in an intense longing. my soul has been drenched
in unreality for so long that i now yearn for something
more, something tangible.

i long for the indispensable realness of your closeness,
your intoxicating warmth, the prolongation of your
hips touching mine, the rich intensity of your desire
overflowing....

i need your beautifully contoured flesh to dance our
naked bodies long and deep into the mythological sky.

i taste everything that is you

i taste your beauty.
i taste your intellect and the infinite depths of your
heart.
i taste your deep silences and your great sorrow.
i taste your hopes for today and every wild dream
   reserved for tomorrow.
i taste your beautiful imperfections and your tireless
   well of self-confidence.
i taste your fury and your calm.
i taste your truth and your inaccuracies.
i taste your purity and your immodest desires.
i taste the softness of your lips and all the kisses yet
   to be given.
i taste your secret heartbeat and the special communion
   that binds our love.
i taste your orgasm as it surges towards me in a
   rich outpouring.

i taste everything that is you.

gateway to madness

i am lying on the bed in that same spot where you had
your delicious ass earlier tonight. my head is pressed
against that spot where nectar erupted like a geyser
from your secret oasis and flowed like liquid fire down
your thighs. my head is there where you held your legs
wide open in such a beautiful immodesty telling me
that this was the gateway to resplendent ascension and
heavy-breathing madness; this was the enchanting place
where all dreams were borne and untempered desires
rage incandescent.

and it is those thoughts that will be my gateway to
sleep tonight, only i will be both sandman and sleeper.
as the one, i will conjure all the images of our moments
together until my eyes close and merge with the dark
stars. as the other, i will dream our passion-scorched
flesh deep into the morning sky.

resurrection

i died just minutes ago,
laid to rest in satin and sweat
as i exhaled my spirit
deep into her welcoming darkness.

and as the moonlight whispers
a benediction of sweet remembrance,
she settles her body close to mine
and wanders a caress
to coax a postmortem rigidity.

the bee keeper

she told me that my words
made her move in that mysterious place,

eloquence dripping off the tip of my tongue
coaxing sweet honey.

i told her that i was merely the bee keeper
cultivating my crop.

my dreams reveal everything

you left me standing there under a cruel, mocking street
light after having been completely dismantled by your
final kiss which descended like a curtain call to this
live action romance now transformed into a tragedy.
standing there, now just a single heartbeat echoing in
the silence with empty hands and empty arms watching
you slowly vanish on the decaying horizon like a dream
sequence gone horribly astray.

now i am in desperate longing for sleep because my
dreams reveal everything that has been denied in my
waking moments. in my dreams, the tendrils of our
boundless desire stretch beyond eternity and the light
of our passion shines brighter than every star in the
sky.

coaxing the waterfall

her body is sublime,
glistening as if in a dream.
the droplets of water
draw a sensual line
marking the path to ecstasy.
she shudders in an unabashed pleasure
and i know that it is my watchful eyes
making her tremble and wet
as she lies back,
eyes shut,
sighing on a plane where flesh meets flesh -
her thighs spread wide
as a finger traces a path
and disappears.
and emerges.
and disappears.
and emerges.
and disappears
in a one finger-inspired waterfall.

cunni

do you ever get restless at night lying in your bed and dream about me with eyes closed and legs wide open? do you ever get so hot that your desire overflows in a tempest and you dream about my tongue immersed in your exquisite aphrodisia, my tongue subdued by your naturally sweetened elixir of the gods? do you dream about my face nestled between your thighs breathing you in, inhaling your intoxicating fragrance? dreaming of me sliding my tongue in and out of your glorious dark - dreaming of me plunging my tongue deep as your hips begin to gyrate and strain upwards as i lick you to the point of climax. only to stop. then start again. stop, start..... moving my tongue back and forth in delicious torment, in sweet excitation until your body shudders in waves of pleasure and you emerge from the dream consumed, delirious, ravenous..... wishing that i was there with you imprisoned in your heat and wetness. my tongue fanning the fire that rages between your legs.

my face wet with the evidence of your coming......

caffeine salvation

every time you take a sip,
        i dream
  i am that cup of coffee
     baptizing
        you in my wetness.

your soft lips
    stained deliciously
       with my caffeine salvation.

that special cup of coffee

last night i dreamt
i was that special cup of coffee,
  and everyday
you would bring your lips near
  kissing me again
    and again
      and again.

cocoa enveloping cocoa
  underneath a moist caffeinated sky.

the magician

   last night i dreamt
i was a magician
and put on a little magic show for you -
     showed you my trick
  of making something disappear
and then reappear.
         disappear.
            reappear...
   all night long.

the perfection of love

the perfection of love is knowing
that in a world so less than perfect,
a world riddled with so much chaos,
ignorance, lack of humanity....
there exists a world so beautiful
unlike any other.
and even though it is an imperfect world,
this world of you and i
is indescribably rich
in its illusion of perfection.

moonlight whispers

it is the middle of the night and i am lying here on my bed. i am alone colored in darkness and bound to a stretch of insomnia that seems unbearably endless. i am alone in this room which has been made unquiet from my constant thoughts of you. thoughts of you have rendered me sleepless. thoughts of you have unmasked my every desire and unleashed a hunger that i can no longer contain and no longer wish to control.

god! i wish you were here with me because i am tired of imaging your closeness. i am tired of imagining your lips, your sweet kisses, your exquisite tongue that interweaves fire into my flesh and transforms my entire being into an ecstatic flame. i don't want to imagine the warmth of your embrace, the intoxication of your wetness, the sweet agony of our bodies entombed in sweat and purified by an all-consuming fire. i don't want to imagine the beautiful echoes of our sighs and the rapturous transfiguration that dances our iridescent flesh into an absolute euphoria.

i do not want just the dream.

i do not want the pain of these imaginings and this incessant longing.

i want you.

a consummate bore

she finds the words
   that i write
 along her sublime interstice
     with the tip of my tongue
a complete bore
   in lieu of the substantial yawning.

the blood that flows

i have been lying here for hours
thinking about you,
about your presence with me earlier tonight
and the way our naked bodies
arranged themselves in such a perfectly wicked
orchestration of desire.

your wandering kisses are still imprinted
on every part of my body.

the scent of our intermingly flesh drenched
in sweat still fills this space.

my cock is still beautifully stained
with the expression of your love that flowed.

manslaughter or suicide?

i died earlier tonight

details of the police report state that i succumbed to
a violent asphyxia, a prolonged liquid immersion as a
result of too much pressure being exerted on the sides of
my head in an apparent attempt to keep me locked in a
particular position until the desired outcome had been
consummated.

the forensics team discovered traces of nectar on the
inner thighs of my assailant which was a direct match to
the substance which was splattered in copious amounts
on my lips and face. and based on that evidence, the
case appeared to be open and shut leading to a swift
conviction for involuntary manslaughter and time
served for the unimaginable suffering that i allegedly
endured.

but what confounded everyone, proving to be a great
mystery was the absence of any indicators synonymous
with a violent asphyxial death. there were no signs of
a struggle, no signs of panic or distress...... only a wide
smile etched on my face as testament of my irrefutable
desire to taste oblivion at any cost - longing to succumb
to a blissful engulfing, surrendering my last breath to a
pleasurable drowning.

i should be working

i should be working but am sitting here at this lonely desk thinking about you. my thoughts keep settling on the last moment in particular when we finally gave in to the insistent beckoning of an insatiable desire - letting that hunger enslave us in the vicissitudes of a raging fire and christen our bodies in a ceremony geared towards an unrestrained devotion of the flesh. i am envisioning that moment with you lying on my bed with legs wide open offering that magical place where you know my tongue likes to linger - that enchanting place where your rich tangy elixir, your rich honeyed flower water excites and nourishes every part of my being. i am lost in the remembrance of our naked bodies wildly colliding and enfolded in the delirium of sweet abandonment and total yieldingness. i am lost in that moment when you wrapped your legs tight around me, our bodies dripping with sweat completely absorbed in an ancient ritual; our naked bodies completely enamored in the exaltation of an unrestrained desire, a rapturous crescendo....

i should working but am sitting here at this lonely desk counting the clock in anticipation of seeing you again - longing to hold you in my arms and do everything that was just whispered to me in my waking dream. only better.

night of wonder

i remember that night when she revealed her lovely flesh to my worshiping eyes. she was stirring, clothed in nothing more than the moonlight's gleam as she lay reposed on the grass underneath the watchful night sky with a salacious look in her eyes and desirous intent inflaming her expressions. there was so much beauty in her every movement - every part of her body exhaled, radiated pure sensuality. she beckoned me closer as her legs slowly began to separate, unfolding like a segment in a beautiful dream. and i relinquished myself to the dream, covering her flesh with that of my own as she guided my entrance with a sigh. our bodies began to move to the rhythm of passionate surrender, stimulated by an uncontrollable hunger, when she whispered in my ear that she wanted to feel the earth tremble; she wanted to see the heavens explode in prismatic colors and distant stars burn and race across the sky.

so i moved out of the way.

baila conmigo

she offered me an apple
in the dark of night
and our movements became rhythmic,
our bodies embracing close
in desire's eternal whisper -
feeling her softness,
her sweet curvatures,
her breath of my face caressing
like a gentle breeze.....

she was beautiful,
ravishing that eternal night
when she offered me an apple
and her seductive hip sway
created movement in me.
as the tempo increased,
our desire began to crescendo
in a sensual harmony,
a melting dream.
and she looked at me
with yearning in her eyes and whispered,
"flow with me."
"baila conmigo."
"flow with me......."
closing my eyes,
i drew her close and became lost
in the passionate fires unfolding.

master puppeteer

she is my beautiful ventriloquist
who manipulates the hidden strings
to transform my every word and gesture
into an echo of her promptings.
she controls every part of me,
using her masterful stagecraft skills
to puppeteer my lips tongue cock
in the most effective manner
to awaken an outpouring of desire.

when she speaks,
i speak eloquently.

when she sighs,
i sigh provocatively.

when she trembles,
i tremble exquisitely.

when she comes,
every part of my wood
is varnished to perfection.

beyond restlessness

i am beyond restlessness
as days blend days
in this same day unending.
i am alone in this space
starring in a one man covid-produced act
set in an empty theater.
my arms are empty.
kisses no longer stain my lips.
the possibility of discerning
even the slightest smile
is lost in the material undercurrents
of the many masks that pass daily.
those inconvenient,
albeit necessary placeholders
where my lips yearn to linger.

-Covid/Lockdown inspired

expectations

i was looking for something more than commonality and manifestations of the customary that pass daily. I wanted someone who would appreciate my uniqueness as an individual rather than estimating my personal worth and depth of character solely on the valuation of my portfolio or the emblem brandishing my car. i wanted someone whose beauty inflamed my mind and encouraged thoughts to linger long after our parting. i wanted someone whose closeness always inspired libidinous inclinations - someone who yearned for my kisses, my insatiable desire, my pleasurable intrusion. i wanted someone whose beauty had the power to invade my dreams and transform every night into an unrestrained bacchanalia where desires runs wild.

she was just looking for bbc.

i guess we were both thoroughly disappointed.

howl

my cock is a wild dog
leashed to an unrestrained desire.
she is the appointed trainer
intent on reinforcing my behavior
for a very specific task.
with every command,
every tantalizing gesture,
i become fashioned into the perfect tool
of obedience shackled to her every whim.
but it is these very same impulses
which stir something dark and primal
awakening the insatiable appetite
of the animal within her.
and the more i rage and howl
under her lascivious demands,
the more she surrenders to the beast.
hungry for my bark.
longing for my bite.

how do you get over a love?

how do you get over a love,
the mad self-forgetting that makes you weak,
makes a fool of you?
i don't think you ever do.
you carry it like baggage until the day you die;
it is a phantasm with words continual on the ear
reminding you of your own personal tragedy
played out in heart's drama.

forced confession

i speak to you in tongues.
it is a systematic interrogation
based on repetition
and uses controlled nonverbal brush strokes
to force your confession -
to hear you utter the words
that i love to hear:
"ooohhhhhh baby!"

3:05 a.m.

i awoke at 3:05a, roused from sleep by an extreme thirst. i had nothing to drink in the house so a short trek to the 24-hour market a few blocks away became an early morning imperative. nevertheless, as soon as i stepped outside of my building.........prostitutes!

prostitutes were everywhere propositioning to anyone and everyone who drove, walked, limped or crawled by. god, how i dreaded this walk as they were set directly in my path. i knew that i would be a prime candidate for their rakish advances in lieu of my aesthetic credentials, but hoped that i would be allowed to pass unmolested. i even cast an earnest prayer, a dire supplication to the heavens imploring the gods for divine intervention. and as my approach drew near, my fretful footsteps creating impact tremors in the pavement, no one uttered a word - silence was fixed on both the arrival and the return! and i spent the rest of the night into the early morning, and many days to follow, burdened by the question why.

the conversation

they sat across from me engaged in a discussion that
exuded a considerable amount of interest considering
not one gazed my way or even affirmed my unquiet
eyes with those of their own. i am not sure how long i
had been sitting there reduced to eavesdropping and a
shameless need for validation, when i heard words of
their conversation accuse someone of being a *typical
arrogant asshole.*

"who could they be talking about?"

that is what i thought - the words ringing, resounding
back and forth in my head.

"who could they be talking about?"

so naturally, curiosity sets my eyes to wander searching
for a person suitable to fit their recriminations, but i see
none. so i look back to my initial point of interest only
to find their eyes all affixed on me.

sculpted in her image

she said that i looked
          like a beautiful statue
          on display in front of her.

heroically posed.
   naked.
        chiseled to perfection.
         intensely silent.
             hard as stone.

a quest for fire

it is well into the deep hour of the night and i am
adrift in my thoughts. i am sitting in this lonely room
tormented, suffering in my thoughts of you. i am
suffering in nostalgic melancholia because i am unable
to contemplate my life without you. i did not want us
to part; all i ever wanted was just you at my side, in
my life. nothing else. nothing else. for the sake of one
more conversation, for the sake of you lying beside me
enfolded in my arms, the touch of your body, the taste
of your lips.... i would throw everything else away. i
love you so much but cannot exist in this space filled
with so much emotional sterility and half-truths -
where love is nothing more than amorous word-play
and not a spontaneous bridge that fuses our disparate
selves into a harmonious whole. existing without a
sense of wholeness and faithfulness. existing without
the rawness of pure abandon, the purity of absolute
consummation. existing without fire......

and what life is this for the moth drawn to the flame
yearning to perish in the fire?

i cannot live without fire.

you cannot live with it.

conversation #1

do you want to come in?
 she said.

yes. but it is pretty dark in there.
 i said.

don't worry. i will be your guide.
 she said.

great! but it also looks pretty damp.
 i said.

it is.
 she said.

do i need to waterproof my items before entering?
 i said.

only if you are afraid of getting soaked.
 she said.

conversation #2

do you want to come in?
 she said.

yes. but it is so dark. how will i find my way?
 i said.

once you enter, it will ignite a flame illuminating the
way for both of us.
 she said.

two vegan cannibals

our bodies are arranged fashionably in decadent op-
position. it is an unscripted and unrestrained sparring
session orchestrated by the intense hunger ravaging our
bodies and geared towards a mutual consummation of
the flesh.

we lick gnaw bite slurp suck devour each other like two
paramecia. there is so much pleasure in this feasting as
we nourish our sinful appetites - drinking from each
other's cup of desire, savoring what each has to offer in
a mutual giving, a mutual engulfing, a sumptuous inter-
change of culinary delights......

i consume her liquid desire to depletion - her creamy
aperitif laden with a superabundance of nectar.

my natural bone broth, doused with generous amounts
of sea salt, satiates her thirst.

beautiful mouth-speak

her beautiful mouth-speak
  is stirring.
i rise to her favor,
        transfixed
  by the sheer eloquence
      of the words
        that she inscribes
on my flesh
      without
        using any words.

fear of flying

you sought merely pleasure in this and perhaps you found it. perhaps not. but i sought nothing and found everything. it is true that everything touches me, but you have touched me in a way that i cannot account. you are so beautiful to me. your beauty has bewitched me and i am in a constant state of intoxication. there is so much richness in your touch, so much warmth in your embrace, pleasure in your soft kisses.... and a day has not passed without my thoughts being fastened on you. a day has not passed where i have not been enchanted by your lovely smile or longed to hear the sound of your voice. every day is spent lost in fantasy wildly dreaming of your alluring flesh and hypnotic curves. every day i am cast on an intense wave of desire yearning for your warm embrace, yearning for the fire of your passion, desiring you as a woman....

and you have no idea how much i want you, how essential you have become to my life. but i cannot let me eyes close more than they have already surrendered. my heart is expanding too much and this i cannot allow - especially when that expansion is a solitary experience which finds me standing alone in the dream that is meant for two. i withdrew because you refuse to come near in any meaningful way and i realized that it was too much to hope for our relationship to evolve into something more, something ever-changing and

ever-growing, something deep. and i realized that what
i needed, the sustenance that i required could not be
found within your embrace. what began with so much
promise, rooted in the joyous nature of our infinite
becoming, had become nothing more than just a mere
placeholder existing surfeit of life with two amorous
vagabonds always destined for replacement.

do you dream about that night?

do you dream about that night - that night with us sitting on the sofa close en rapt in conversation, gazing deep into each other's eyes? do you remember your hand in mine, my hand softly caressing yours, the space between us slowly decreasing, a fresh desire awakening as a love song began to unfold?

do you dream about that night as i pulled you close, resting my lips lightly on yours like a surreptitious prayer and the soft kisses that were whispered with such eloquence - the soft kisses, the sweet kisses that were exchanged in such a beautiful evocation of breath, lips, tongue transporting us to a new level of wanting?

do you remember standing in the middle of the living room completely absorbed in the delights found within each other's embrace - the way we kissed each other with such passion, such hunger as our tongues connected in such a beautiful echo, a mellifluous song? do you remember the throbbing ache swelling between my legs, the insistent wetness flowing between yours, an impatience to further explore this land of physical gratification?

do you dream about that night as we made our way into the kitchen? the moonlight was dancing in the dark sky, tree branches were silently whispering, the constant hum of the refrigerator behind us serenading as we stood in the kitchen kissing fiercely, drunkenly, lost in the sweet inebriation of a raging sexual appetite - standing there ache against ache, our bodies pressed tight together, my body hard against your

softness, my desire growing in inches as your hips became
all sexy provocation and immodest undulation. your little
black skirt inching higher and higher above your gorgeous
ass. your anxious nipples straining against the material. your
head falling back on my shoulder. your long beautiful hair
astride my face....

do you dream about that entrancing night when i lowered
you onto the satin sheets and covered you with my body?
my naked flesh enveloping yours, our hearts beating one
against the other, our breath morphing into sighs. do you
dream about that portion of my flesh giving anything to feel
me inside you once again? do you remember the hunger,
the expectancy, the urgency as you lay there with legs bent
upwards and hips straining, your legs wide open in a capti-
vating invitation as i entered you slow, breathtakingly slow,
teasingly slow? and you watched me going in and coming
out in a beautiful dream, a perfect dream of yieldingness,
completeness and moisture-kissed communion as the waters
of a divine quickening flowed in a lavish unity leaving us
thoroughly nourished, enshrouded in steam and sweat, lost
in the rapturous dreaming.

where words fail

there is no metaphor,
  no euphemism
    or syntactical refinement
which even comes close
to expressing
that perfect moment
of being close
  to your heartbeat
    and immersed
      in your spellbinding wetness.

unsung kisses

we are a mist
of unsung kisses
floating on a lonesome drift
waiting to coalesce
into a dream
of soft-lulling caresses
and incandescent flesh.

underneath my watching

underneath my balcony,
a beautiful distraction
with sun-kissed hair
and wind-divined curvatures
summons my watching.

she gazes upward
in awareness of my devotion
and offers a smile in passing,
providing the inspiration
for these simple words.

fee-fi-fo-fum

the restless seeds
of my desire have sprouted
a magical beanstalk,
erected in anticipation
of your spirited climb
and the many splendors
that await among the clouds.

inked remembrance

your echoing sighs
     and ardent wetness....
the way your body speaks to me
   in this enraptured
      transference of desire -
offering
   very
      delicious
         unspoken
            words
that will reverberate
   in inked-remembrance
      long after the separation
         of our smoldering flesh.

a truth about love

love is not an ascension from primal desires and un-
holy indiscretions that have been absolved by the gods
and blessed by some kind of celestial governance.

love is not a magical transportation into a buoyant,
beautiful fairy-tale realm where only fascination and
wonder exists - where majestic unicorns frolic and the
sky is always an eternal blue.

love is nothing more than an instability of the senses,
a deviation into temporary madness, a repudiation
of your unique self for the illusory promise of eternal
bliss and unwavering devotion. love is not a glorious
emancipation from incompleteness or a divine elixir
to remedy a spiritual and physiological flaw. love is
just an uninspired euphemism engineered to transcend
the primal nature of desire by sublimating the vulgar
and immoral into the respectable and ideal. love is an
additive, the unnecessary msg coloring your already
tasty kung pao chicken.

love is just a gossamer veil, a very thin coating that
sits on top of the raw, devouring flame of lust. and it
is this flame that consumes, nourishes, transcends....
always leaving us yearning for more.

beautiful refuge

these brief moments with you, the infusion of life that
you give me in the form of sweet kisses paint a veil
over this incomprehensible society - this modernism
of pure madness and its obsessive romanticization of
ignorance.

your kisses have become the remedy, the necessary
vaccine.

your soft kisses are my beautiful refuge that always
counteracts the ugly waking.

snake charmer

she comes near with all of her sexy allurements, this
lovely vision laying bare her tantalizing instruments
specifically tuned to coax me from my hiding place.

as her hips begin to sway in a sensual harmony, the
coiled slumberous serpent awakens and begins to rise -
only to be frozen in upward suspension by the rhythmic
splendor of her seductive hip gyrations which inspires
certain impulses and radiates the madness that i crave.

it is a mutual longing that connects us, binds us as
my movements start to align with hers. she takes the
serpent in hand with no nervousness and directs my
flickering tongue to the location targeted by desire's
indispensable needs. her breath quickens, her chest
heaves, sweet honey-suckle begins to flow as she melts
and sighs in an unabashed pleasure - enthralled by my
fervent slithering, subdued by my venom as i wrap her
from the inside.

perhaps

perhaps i am tasting what no one else has.

perhaps not.

i realize that it is sheer arrogance or extreme naivety
to think that i am the first person to drink from your
cup of desire.

but what i know to be true, is that at this particular
moment, this special elixir of yours now being presented
has been cultivated especially for me.

acknowledgments

*i have wandered many miles and crossed several
oceans in search of truth, meaning, beauty, love.....
i have witnessed so much wonderment, so many
breathtaking sights; i have stood at the footsteps of
the marvelous and been completely ensorcelled and
humbled by the sheer immensity of it all.*

*and what i have discovered is that there is nothing
more wondrous, more precious, more marvelous
than the love of a mother.*

nothing.

*thank you mom.
for the love, for all the sacrifices, everything.....*

www.ingramcontent.com/pod-product-compliance
Lightning Source LLC
Chambersburg PA
CBHW021210130726
47988CB00002B/595